# Exmoor

■ Exmoor is an area of great beauty with many places of interest and natural attractions.

■ This new publication contains Ordnance Survey 'Explorer' maps in a convenient book format with a useful index to the main attractions of the Exmoor National Park. It is the essential companion when exploring, showing all footpaths, rights of way and public access land.

## CONTENTS

### Geographers' A-Z Map Company Limited

Fairfield Road, Borough Green,
Sevenoaks, Kent TN15 8PP
Telephone: 01732 781000 (Enquiries & Trade Sales)
          01732 783422 (Retail Sales)
www.az.co.uk
Copyright © Geographers' A-Z Map Company Limited
EDITION 1   2014

Ordnance Survey

This product includes mapping data licensed from Ordnance Survey® with the permission of the Controller of Her Majesty's Stationery Office.

Mapping contents © Crown copyright and database rights 2013 Ordnance Survey 100017302

# Communications

## ROADS AND PATHS
Not necessarily rights of way

|  |  |
|---|---|
| Ⓢ Ⓢ | Service Areas |
| **7** | Junction number |
| M I or A 6(M) | Motorway |
| A 35 | Dual carriageway |
| A 30 | Main road |
| B 3074 | Secondary road |
| | Narrow road with passing places |
| | Road under construction |
| | Road generally more than 4m wide |
| | Road generally less than 4m wide |
| | Other road, drive or track, fenced and unfenced |
| ≫ → | Gradient: steeper than 20% (1 in 5); 14% (1 in 7) to 20% (1 in 5) |
| Ferry | Ferry; Ferry P – passenger only |
| .................... | Path |

## RAILWAYS

|  |  |
|---|---|
| | Multiple track standard gauge |
| | Single track standard gauge |
| | Narrow gauge or Light rapid transit system (LRTS) and station |
| | Road over; road under; level crossing |
| | Cutting; tunnel; embankment |
| | Station, open to passengers; siding |

## PUBLIC RIGHTS OF WAY

|  |  |
|---|---|
| ----------- Footpath | ————— Bridleway |
| +++++++ | Byway open to all traffic |
| ╾┼╾┼╾┼╾ | Restricted byway (not for use by mechanically propelled vehicles) |

Public rights of way shown on this map have been taken from local authority definitive maps and later amendments. Rights of way are liable to change and may not be clearly defined on the ground.
Please check with the relevant local authority for the latest information.

The representation on this map of any other road, track or path is no evidence of the existence of a right of way.

## OTHER PUBLIC ACCESS

|  |  |
|---|---|
| • • • | Other routes with public access (not normally shown in urban areas) |

The exact nature of the rights on these routes and the existence of any restrictions may be checked with the local highway authority. Alignments are based on the best information available.

|  |  |
|---|---|
| ◆ ◆ 🔔 | National Trail |
| ◆ ◆ ◆ | Long Distance Route and Recreational Route |
| - - - - - - - - | Permissive footpath |
| — — — — — | Permissive bridleway |

Footpaths and bridleways along which landowners have permitted public use but which are not rights of way. The agreement may be withdrawn.

|  |  |
|---|---|
| • • • | Traffic-free cycle route |
| ▢1 | National cycle network route number – traffic free |
| ■1 | National cycle network route number – on road |

Firing and test ranges in the area. Danger! Observe warning notices

Visit www.access.mod.uk for information

## ACCESS LAND

Portrayal of access land on this map is intended as a guide to land which is normally available for access on foot, for example access land created under the Countryside and Rights of Way Act 2000, and land managed by the National Trust, Forestry Commission and Woodland Trust. Access for other activities may also exist. Some restrictions will apply; some land will be excluded from open access rights.
The depiction of rights of access does not imply or express any warranty as to its accuracy or completeness. Observe local signs and follow the Countryside Code.

Visit www.countrysideaccess.gov.uk for up-to-date information

|  |  |
|---|---|
| | Access land boundary and tint |
| | Access land in woodland area |
| 🛈 | Access information point |
| MANAGED ACCESS | Access permitted within managed controls for example, local bylaws |

Visit www.access.mod.uk for information

# General Information

## BOUNDARIES

|  |  |
|---|---|
| — ┼ — ┼ — | National |
| — · — · — · — | County (England) |
| — — — — | Unitary Authority (UA), Metropolitan District (Met Dist), London Borough (LB) or District (Scotland & Wales are solely Unitary Authorities) |
| · · · · · · · · · · · | Civil Parish (CP) (England) or Community (C) (Wales) |
| | National Park boundary |

## VEGETATION

Limits of vegetation are defined by positioning of symbols

|  |  |  |  |
|---|---|---|---|
|  | Coniferous trees | | |
| | Non-coniferous trees | | |
| | Coppice | | |
|  | Bracken, heath or rough grassland | ◇◇◇◇ | Orchard |
|  | Marsh, reeds or saltings | | Scrub |

## GENERAL FEATURES

| | | | | | |
|---|---|---|---|---|---|
| + | Place of worship | △ ⊼ | Triangulation pillar; mast | BP/BS | Boundary post/stone |
| | Current or former place of worship | | Windmill, with or | CG | Cattle grid |
| ▮ | with tower | ⋇ | without sails | CH | Clubhouse |
| ▮ | with spire, minaret or dome | ⊺ ⊺ | Wind pump; wind turbine | FB | Footbridge |
| ▢ ▭ | Building; important building | pylon pole | Electricity transmission line | MP ; MS | Milepost; milestone |
| ▨ | Glasshouse | ⊪⊪⊪⊪ | Slopes | Mon | Monument |
| ▲ | Youth hostel | Gravel pit    Sand pit | | PO | Post office |
| ▪ | Bunkhouse/camping barn/other hostel | | | Pol Sta | Police station |
| ⬗ | Bus or coach station | | | Sch | School |
| | | | | TH | Town hall |
| 里 里 人 | Lighthouse; disused lighthouse; beacon | Other pit or quarry | Landfill site or slag/spoil heap | NTL | Normal tidal limit |
| | | | | ∘W; Spr | Well; spring |

## HEIGHTS AND NATURAL FEATURES

52 ·   Ground survey height

284 ·   Air survey height

Surface heights are to the nearest metre above mean sea level. Where two heights are shown, the first height is to the base of the triangulation pillar and the second (in brackets) to the highest natural point of the hill.

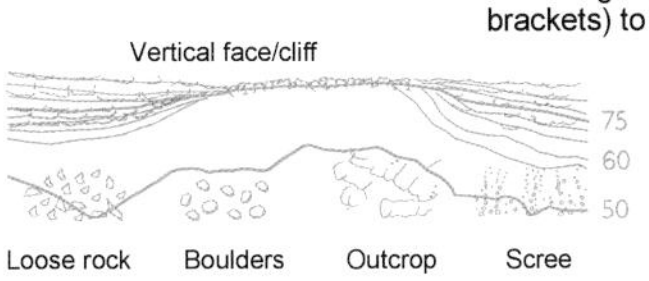

Vertical face/cliff

Loose rock    Boulders    Outcrop    Scree

75
60
50

Contours may be at 5 or 10 metres vertical interval

Water

Mud

Sand; sand & shingle

## ARCHAEOLOGICAL AND HISTORICAL INFORMATION

| | | | | |
|---|---|---|---|---|
| ⁜ | Site of antiquity | ∗ ⊪⊪⊪ | Visible earthwork | Information provided by English Heritage for England and the Royal Commissions on the Ancient and Historical Monuments for Scotland and Wales |
| ⚔ 1066 | Site of battle (with date) | VILLA | Roman | |
| | | Castle | Non-Roman | |

## Selected Tourist and Leisure Information

| | | | | | | | |
|---|---|---|---|---|---|---|---|
| P | Parking | 人 | Camp site | 🚲 | Cycle hire | ⚲ | Fishing |
| P&R | Park & Ride, - all year | 🚐 | Caravan site | U | Horse riding | ☆ | Other tourist feature |
| P&R | - seasonal | ⓚ | Recreation leisure sports centre | ⚠ | Viewpoint | ✝ | Cathedral/Abbey |
| i | Information cen. - all year | ⚑ | Golf course or links | ✕ | Picnic site | IMI | Museum |
| i | - seasonal | 亞 | Theme pleasure park | � | Country park | 🏰 | Castle/fort |
| V | Visitor centre | 🚂 | Preserved railway | ❀ | Garden arboretum | 🏛 | Building of historic interest |
| 🅰 | Forestry Commission visitor centre | 🍺 | Public house/s | ⚓ | Water activities | HC | Heritage centre |
| PC | Public convenience | 🎨 | Craft centre | ⛵ | Slipway | 📛 | National Trust |
| 📞 | Telephone - public | ❗ | Walks/trails | 🛥 | Boat trips | 🔲 | English Heritage |
| 📞 | - roadside assistance | 🚲 | Cycle trail | ⚓ | Boat hire | ◈ | World Heritage site/area |
| 📞 | - emergency | 🚴 | Mountain bike trail | 🦆 | Nature reserve | | |

1 Kilometre = 0.6214 mile
1 metre = 3.2808 feet

## Scale 1:25 000

1 mile = 1.6093 kilometres
100 feet = 30.48 metres

1000 m          0          1 km

3000 feet        0          1/2 mile

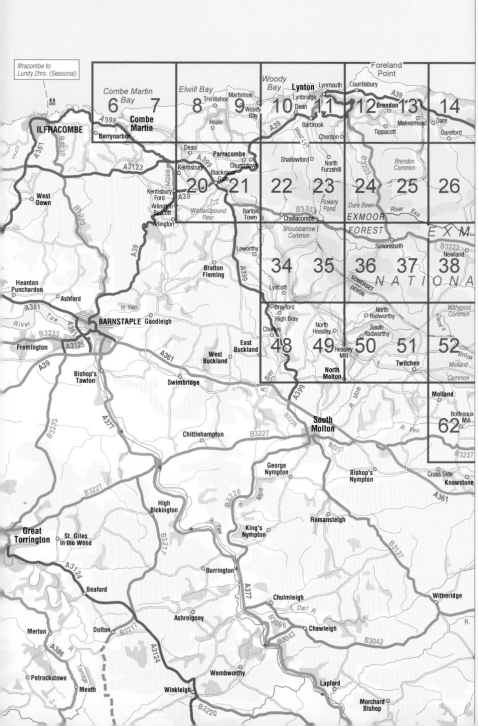

BRISTOL

Ilfracombe to
Lundy 2hrs. (Seasonal)

Combe Martin
Bay

**6** **7**

Combe
Martin

Elwill Bay

**8** **9**

Woody
Bay

**10**

Lynton

Lynmouth

**11**

Foreland
Point

**12** **13**

Countisbury

Brendon

**14**

Oare

Oareford

ILFRACOMBE

Berrynarbor

Trentishoe
Martinhoe

Heale

Woody
Bay

Lynbridge
Dean

Barbrook

Cheriton

A39

Malmsmead

Tippacott

West
Down

Dean

Kentisbury

Parracombe
Churchtown

Blackmoor
Gate

**20** **21**

Kentisbury
Ford

Arlington
Beccott

Arlington

Wistlandpound
Resr.

Barton
Town

**22** **23**

Shallowford

North
Furzehill

Challacombe

Pinkery
Pond

**24** **25**

Dure Down

Brendon
Common

River Exe

**26**

EXMOOR

FOREST

EX M

Heanton
Punchardon

Ashford

BARNSTAPLE

Goodleigh

R. Yeo

Bratton
Fleming

Leworthy

**34** **35**

Lydcott

Shoulsbarrow
Common

Simonsbath

SOMERSET
DEVON

**36** **37**

**38**

Newland

B3223

N A T I O N A

Withypool
Common

Dane's

Fremington

River

Taw

B3233

A361

A3125

Bishop's
Tawton

Swimbridge

West
Buckland

East
Buckland

**48**

Brayford
High Bray

Charles

**49**

North
Heasley

North
Molton

Heasley
Mill

North
Radworthy

South
Radworthy

**50** **51**

Twitchen

**52**

Molland
Common

Brook

Molland

**62**

Bottreaux
Mill

Chittlehampton

B3227

South
Molton

B3227

B3226

R. Mole

R. Yeo

B3227

Cross Side

Knowstone

A361

Great
Torrington

St. Giles
in the Wood

B3227

High
Bickington

George
Nympton

King's
Nympton

R. Mole

R. Taw

Romansleigh

Bishop's
Nympton

B3137

Beaford

A3124

Burrington

A377

Chulmleigh

Witheridge

Merton

Dolton

B3217

Ashreigney

Chawleigh

L. Dart R.

B3042

B3042

A386

Petrockstowe

Meeth

Torridge R.

A3124

Winkleigh

Wembworthy

B3220

Lapford

Morchard
Bishop

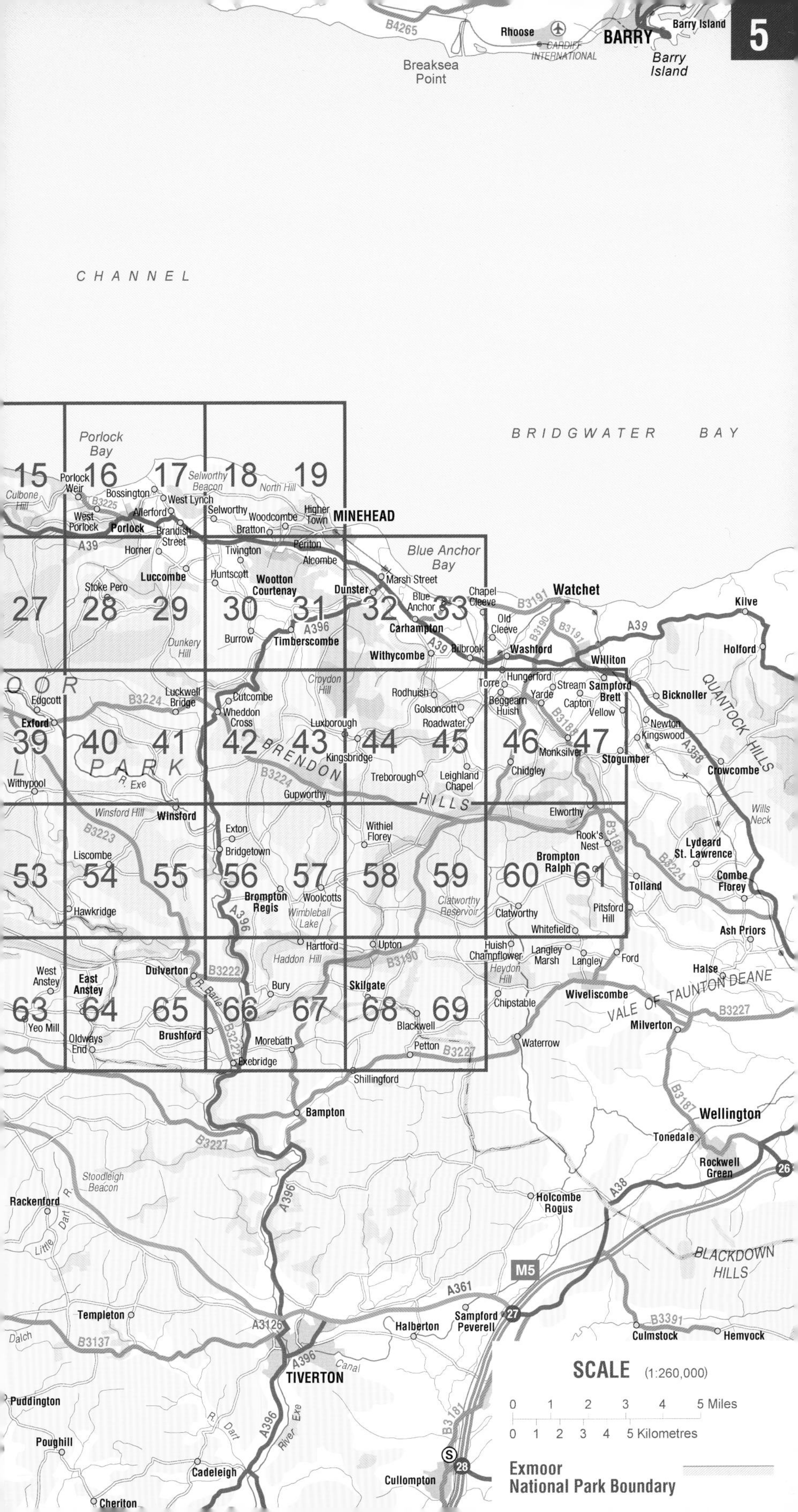
B4265
Rhoose
CARDIFF INTERNATIONAL
BARRY
Barry Island
Barry Island
Breaksea Point
CHANNEL
BRIDGWATER BAY
Porlock Bay
15
16
17
18
19
Culbone Hill
Porlock Weir
Bossington
Selworthy Beacon
North Hill
West Lynch
B3225
West Porlock
Allerford
Porlock
Brandish Street
Selworthy
Woodcombe
Higher Town
MINEHEAD
Bratton
A39
Horner
Tivington
Periton
Alcombe
Blue Anchor Bay
Marsh Street
Luccombe
Huntscott
Stoke Pero
Wootton Courtenay
Dunster
27
28
29
30
31
32
33
Chapel Cleeve
Watchet
Kilve
Blue Anchor
B3191
Old Cleeve
A396
Carhampton
B3190
A39
Burrow
Timberscombe
Dunkery Hill
Withycombe
Bilbrook
Washford
Holford
Williton
Croydon Hill
Torre
Hungerford
Rodhuish
Stream
Sampford Brett
Bicknoller
QUANTOCK HILLS
OOR
Luckwell Bridge
Cutcombe
Beggearn Huish
Yarde
Capton
Edgcott
B3224
Wheddon Cross
Golsoncott
Vellow
Exford
Luxborough
Roadwater
B3188
Newton
Kingswood
39
40
41
42
43
44
45
46
47
A358
L
PARK
BRENDON
Kingsbridge
Monksilver
Stogumber
Crowcombe
Withypool
R. Exe
B3224
Treborough
Leighland Chapel
Chidgley
Gupworthy
HILLS
Elworthy
Wills Neck
Winsford Hill
Winsford
Exton
Withiel Florey
B3188
Rook's Nest
Lydeard St. Lawrence
B3223
Liscombe
Bridgetown
Brompton Ralph
53
54
55
56
57
58
59
60
61
B3224
Combe Florey
Tolland
Brompton Regis
Woolcotts
Clatworthy Reservoir
Hawkridge
Wimbleball Lake
Clatworthy
Pitsford Hill
A396
Whitefield
Ash Priors
Hartford
Upton
Huish Champflower
Langley Marsh
Langley
Ford
Haddon Hill
B3190
West Anstey
East Anstey
Dulverton
B3222
Heydon Hill
Halse
Bury
Skilgate
VALE OF TAUNTON DEANE
Wiveliscombe
R. Barle
Chipstable
63
64
65
66
67
68
69
B3227
Yeo Mill
Oldways End
Brushford
B3222
Morebath
Blackwell
Milverton
Petton
B3227
Waterrow
Exebridge
Shillingford
Bampton
B3187
Wellington
B3227
Tonedale
Rockwell Green
26
Stoodleigh Beacon
Rackenford
Little Dart R.
A396
A38
Holcombe Rogus
BLACKDOWN HILLS
M5
A361
Templeton
Sampford Peverell
27
A3126
Halberton
B3391
Culmstock
Hemyock
Dalch
B3137
A396
Canal
TIVERTON
SCALE (1:260,000)
0 1 2 3 4 5 Miles
0 1 2 3 4 5 Kilometres
Puddington
R. Dart
A396
River Exe
B3181
Poughill
S
28
Cadeleigh
Cullompton
Exmoor National Park Boundary
Cheriton

1

51

2

1 50

3

C h a n n e l

49

8 The

Blackstone
Point

Rawn's
Rocks

Blackstone
Beach                                                    Red
                                                         Cleave
MLW

The Rawn's                                    Waterfall        4

                    Great
                    Hangman
                    Cairn                                         Holdstone
East                              Girt Down                        Down
Challacombe          South West                  Sherrycombe
Farm        318      Tarka Trail  Coast Path                      Holdstone Hill   Sto
                                                                 349
                                                                  Stones
            Girt Farm

Netherton                                                                         5

            Girt                                              Holdstone
Knap Down   Down                                              Farm               47
            Farm       COMBE MARTIN CP
Silver Dale        232    Standing
Nurseries                 Stone
                    237
Silver Mines  Chy
Farm          Mines
              (dis)                          Vellacot Lane  263              Ve
                                                            273              6
Comers                                                           270

Skirhead                    Beara
Farm              Buzzacott Manor
                  House        Coulscott                     Stony
                                                             Corner
46

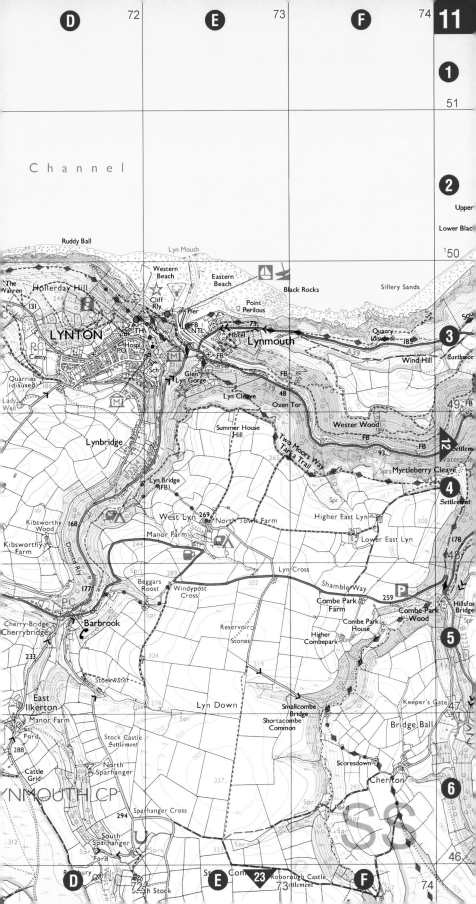

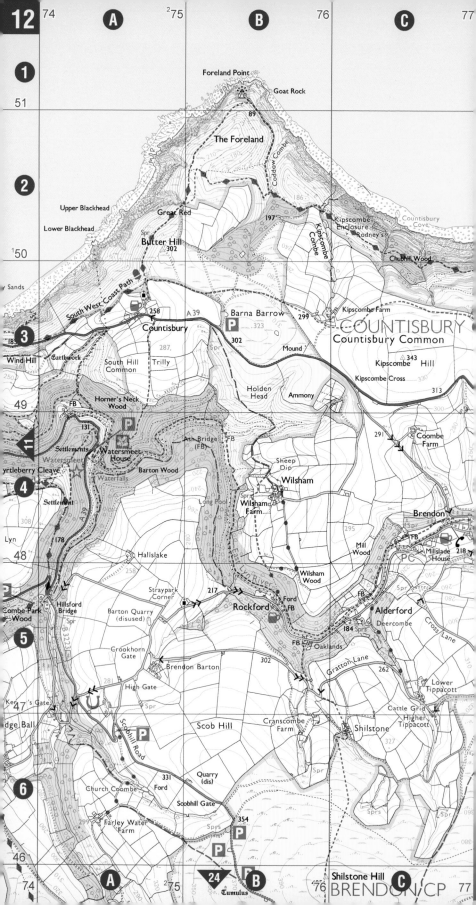

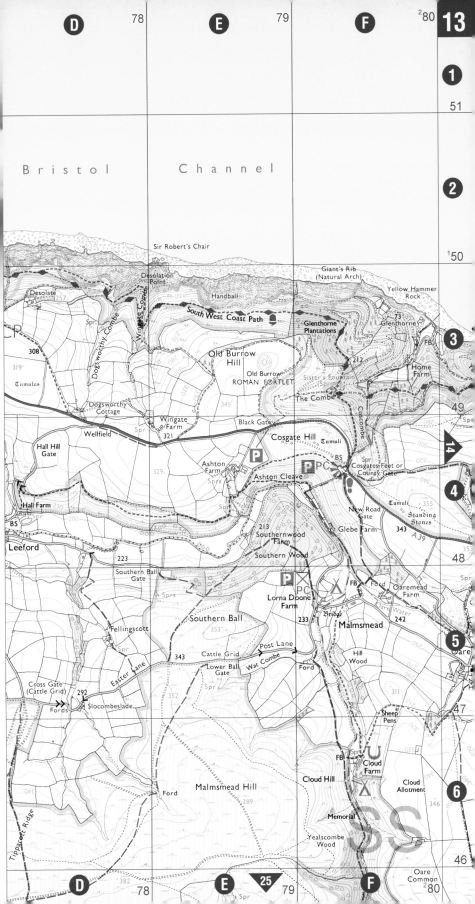

**16**

86　**A**　87　**B**　88　**C**　89

**1**
51

**2**
¹50

B r i s t o l

**3**

49

**15**

Porlock Bay

ore Point

**4**

Th...le

Bossington Beach

Worthy

Dock　Groynes

Pipe Line

⁴48

Memorial

ombe

Quay

Submarine Forest

Vorthy Wood

B 3225

P
PC

Porlock Beach

Groynes

Butchers
Plantation

Porlock
Weir

Hotel

Porlockford
Bridge

Sparkhayes Lane

South West Coast Path

**5**

Porlockford

West Porlock

Spr

Eastcott
Bridge

Hawknest Combe

ott Lane

15

Birchanger
Bridge

Porlockford Combe

⁴47

B 3225

P

Spr

Greencombe

Broom
Close

25

V

Sparkhayes

Birchanger

Ford

Toll

New Rd

Allerpark
Combe

Court
Place

Libry

PO

Sch

Do

Combe Meadow

The Parks

**6**

PC

Porlock

High
Dove

Reservoir

Hawkcombe

Porlock Hill

Halse Combe

Halsecombe
House

Cem

Reservoir

350

252

Cattle
Grid

Doverhay

300

P
347

Cattle
Grid

350

**A**

**28**

ebush

**B**

Peep-out

**C**

Glen
Lodge

86

Comb

Ford

87

FB

143

Ford

88

89

**1**

51

**2**

¹50

C h a n n e l

**3**

49

Greenaleigh Point

Greenaleigh
Sand

**4**

Spr

Culver Cliff Sand

48

Greenaleigh
Farm

Culver Cliff

Mean Low Water

**P**!

Moor
Wood

199

Mean High Water

**P** **P**C

**5**

SWC Path

Beacon

IRB Sta

Wood Combe

Harbour

47

Reservoir

Higher Moor
Fm

Higher Town

Mon

**P**

Lower
Moor
Fm

48

**MINEHEAD**

Woodcombe

White
Cross

33

The Strand
Breakwaters

**PC** **V**

**6**

65

Sch

West Somerset Railway

7

Hospl

26

Cemy

Liby

46

Mount
Periton

**D** 96     **E** **31** 97     **F** 98

School

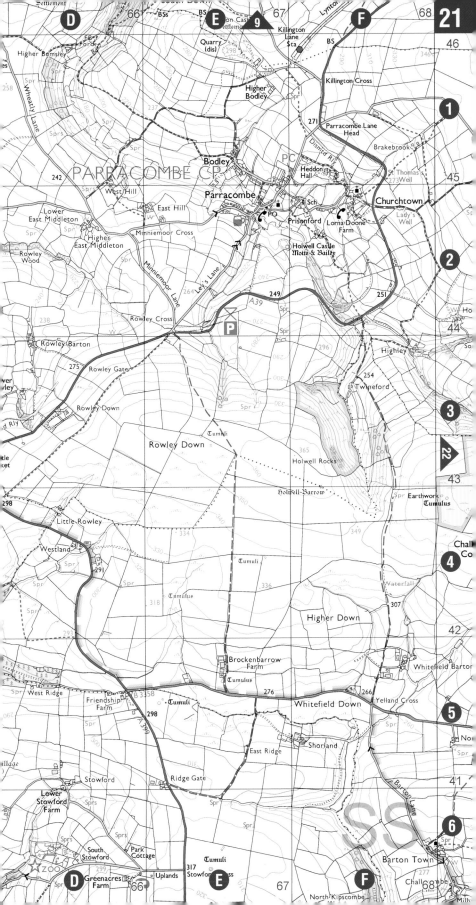

68 A 69 B 70 C 71

Wool**10**er Co**B**on

Barham Hill

Thornworthy

46

325

346

The Lodge

Ford

281

Ford

1

352

Woolhanger Farm

268

302

45

334

Thorn

Lady's Well

Woolhanger Wood

Henge

Parracombe Common

South Common

Spr

Settlement

Tumulus

Cannon Hill

2

368

Sheep Dip

Roe Barrow

Butter Hill

Holworthy

Higher Holworthy

370

380

400

Spr

410

44

Southlands Wood

430

Spr

470

ley

460

Chapman Barrows

3

Two Gates

Memorial

480

470

21

Stone Setting

43

Earthwork

Tumulus

Spr

Long Stone

Tumuli

470

Tumulus

Radworthy

Longstone Barrow

475

4

Challacombe Common

Spr

400

Swincombe Rocks

Cairns

Tumulus

Stone Setting

390

Withycombe

356

380

370

360

Bray Reservoir

42

Whitefield Barton

CHALLACOMBE CP

357

Yarbury Combe

Launchett's Ground

330

Ford

North Regis Common

North Swincombe

South Swincombe

Spr

5

287 Withecombe Gate

Ford

Twitchen

North Lane

North Barton

River Bray

326

369

Spr

Barton Gate

PO

Old Close

278

255

326

41

312

Challacombe

Old Close Bottom

Old Close Quarry (disused)

275

Barton Plantation

W

South Lane (Track)

South Regis Common

6

300

Spr

Town

246

Rooksfoot Bridge

Sheep Dip

335

Chall

W

68

A

69

**34**

B

70

C

Mill Bridge

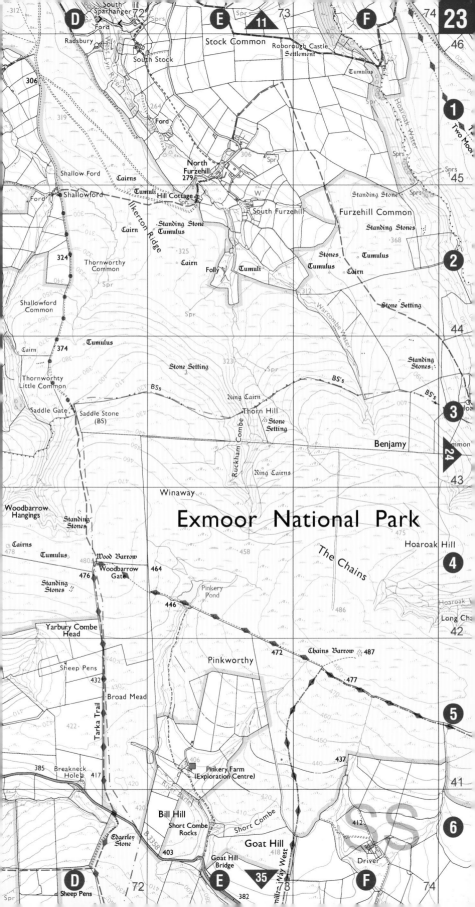

# Exmoor National Park

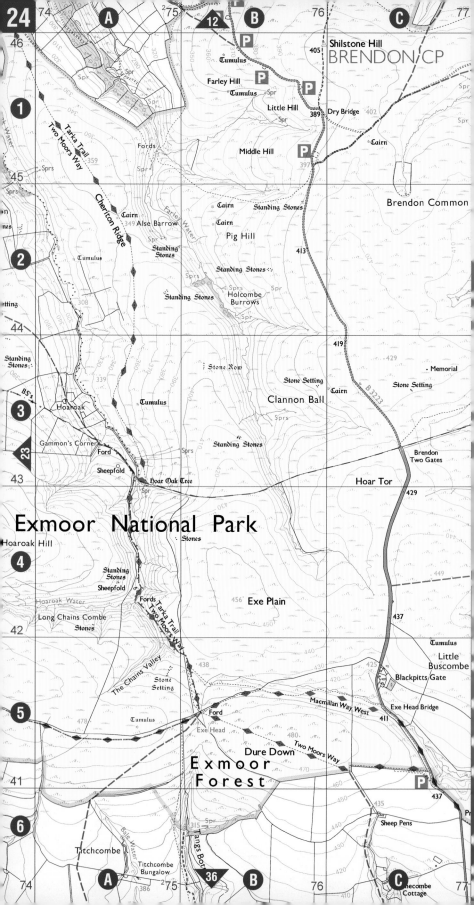

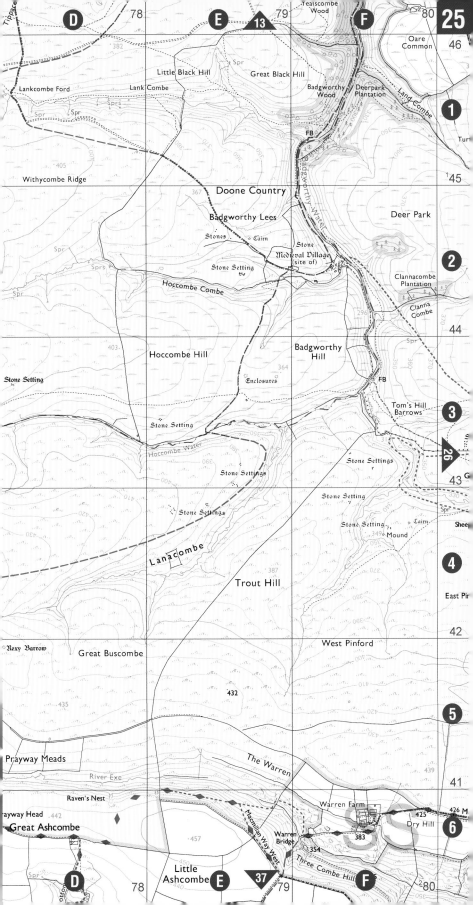

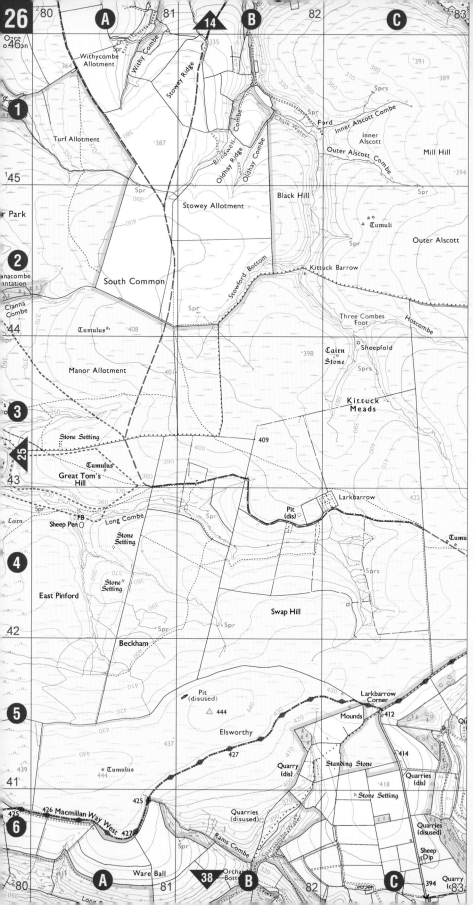

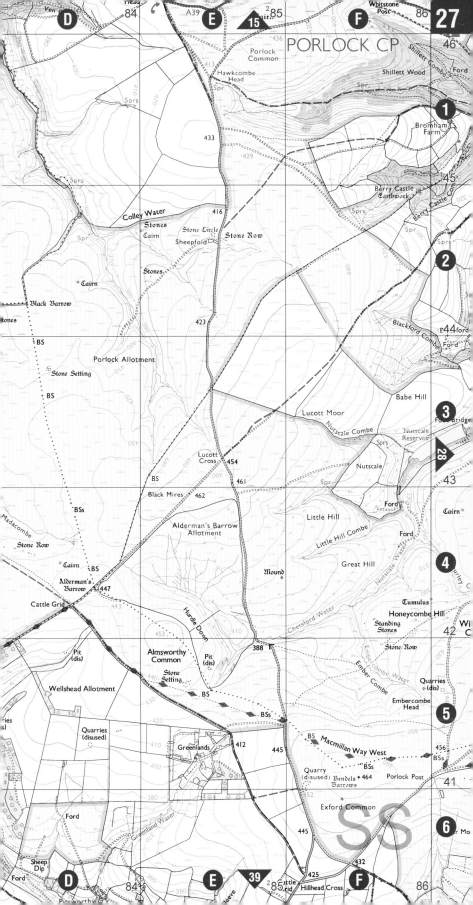

PORLOCK CP

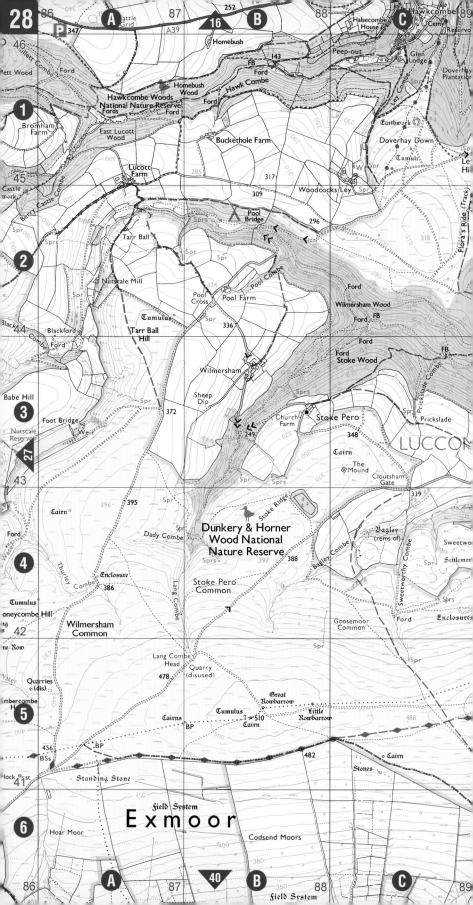

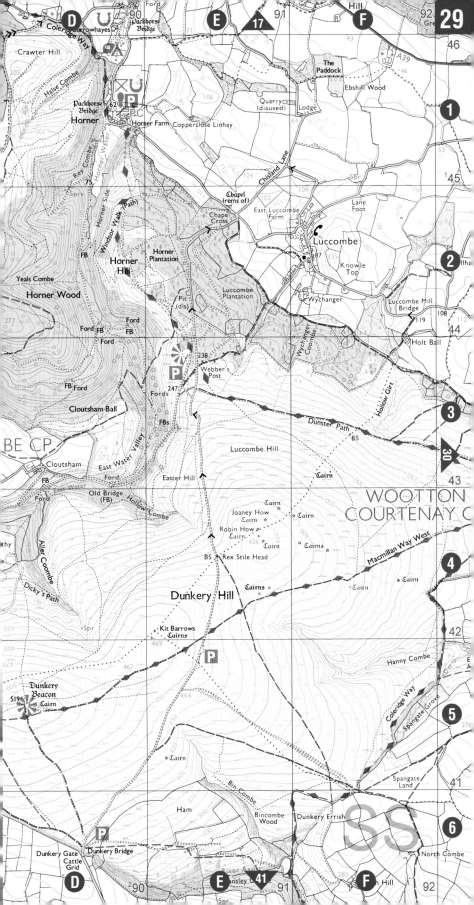

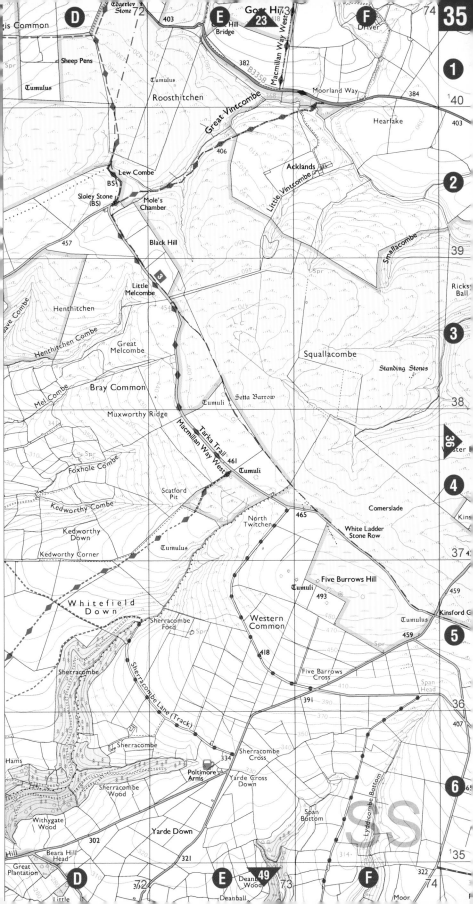

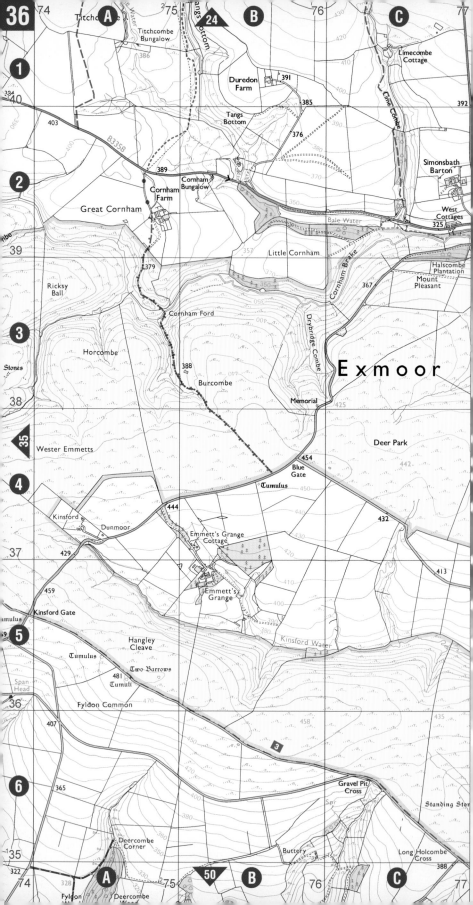

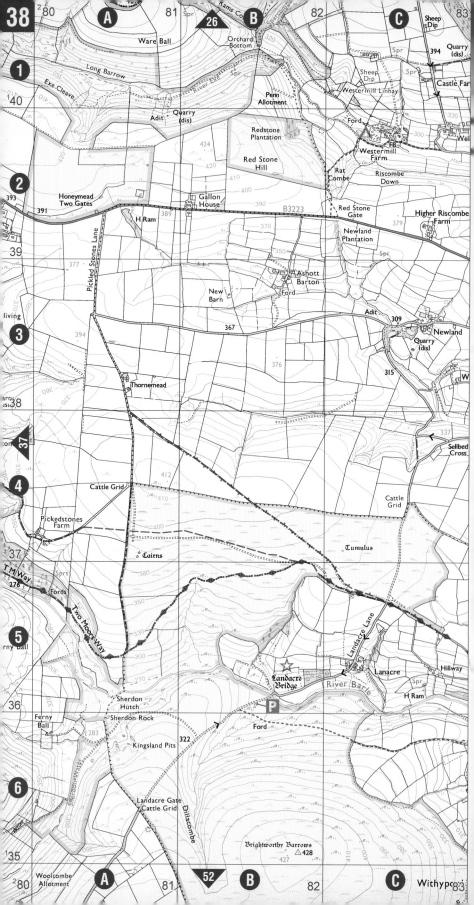

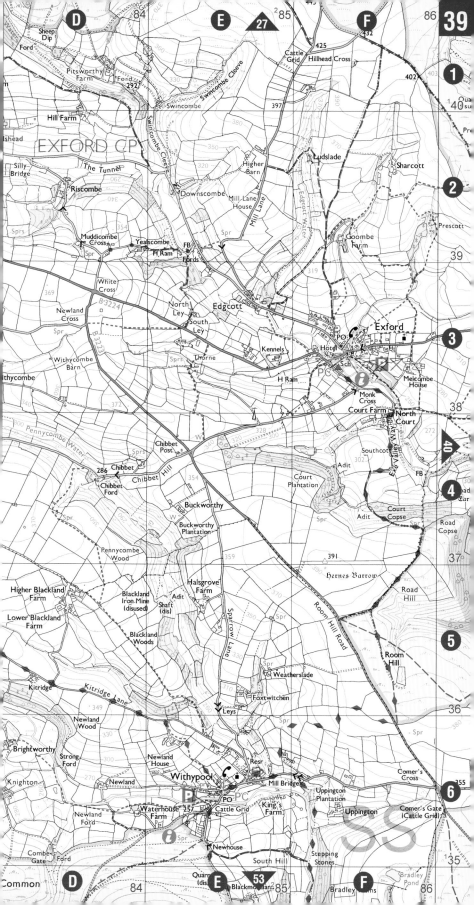

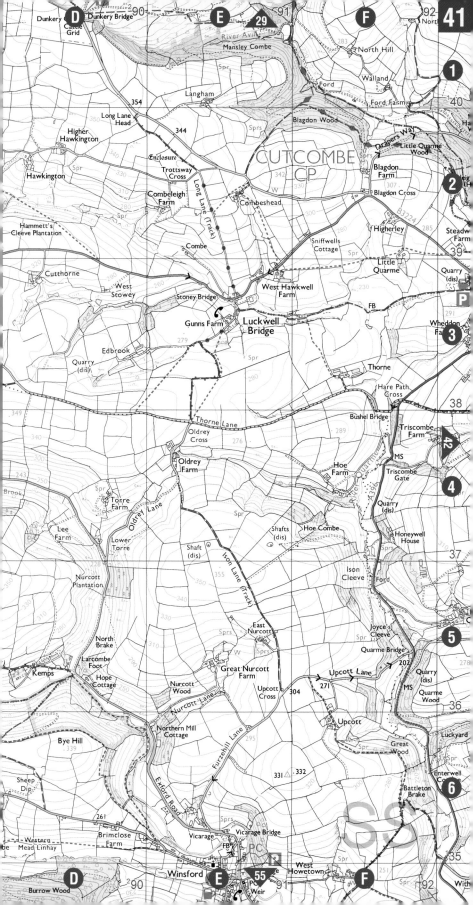

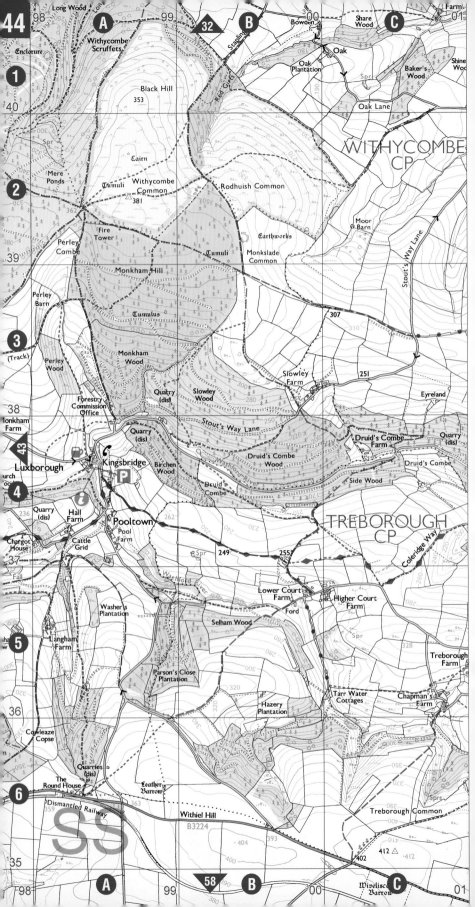

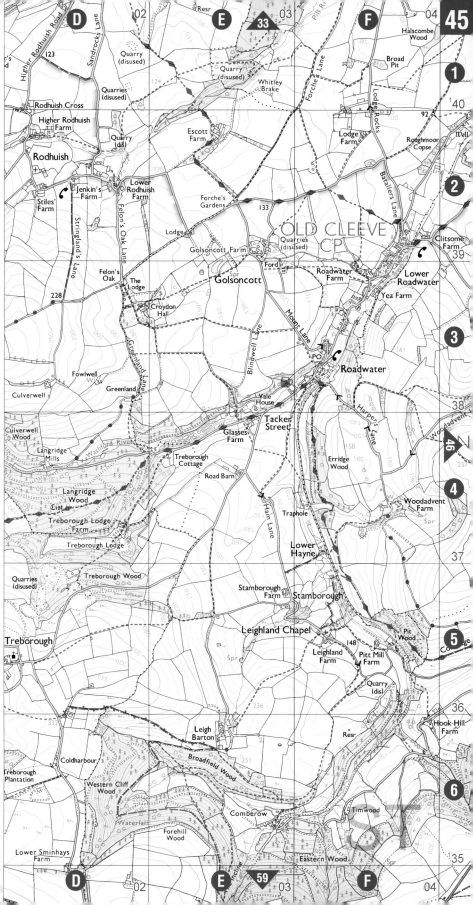

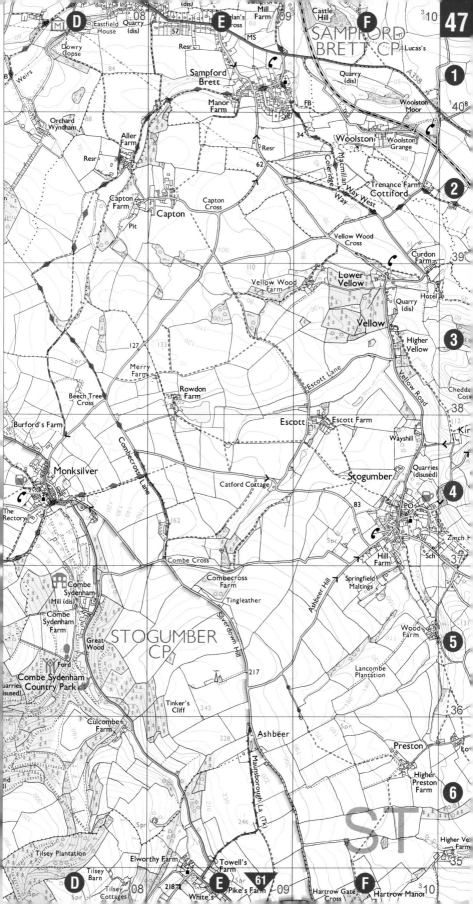

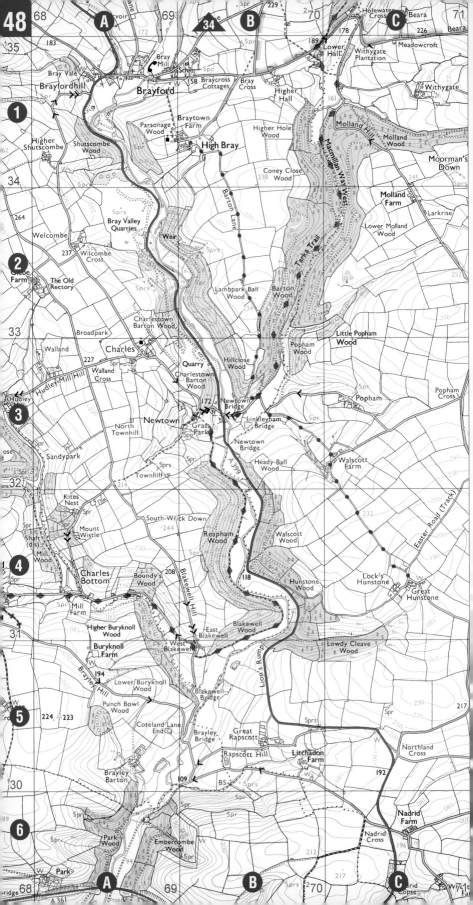

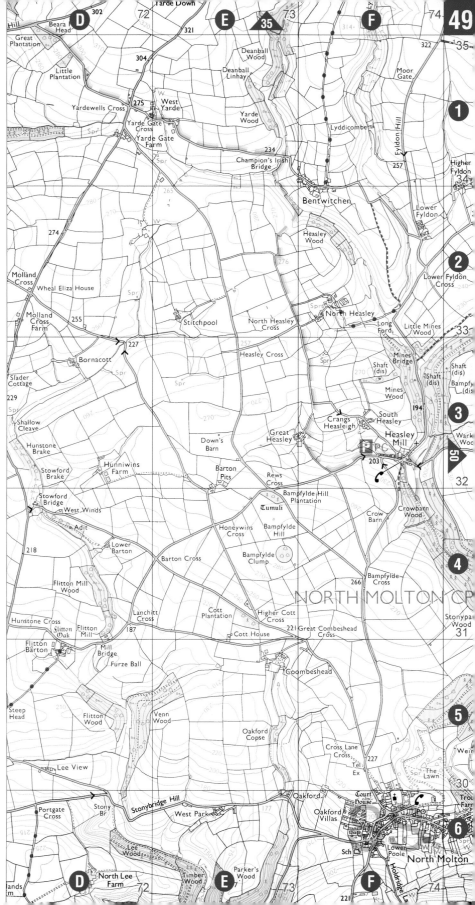

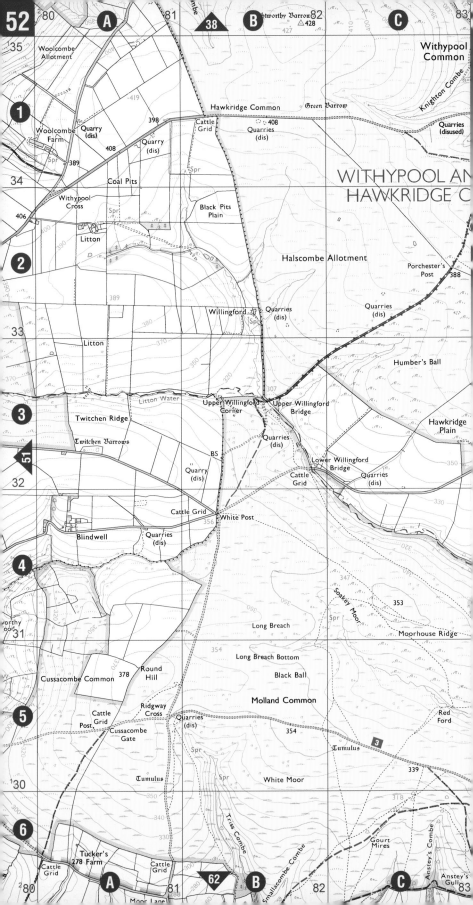

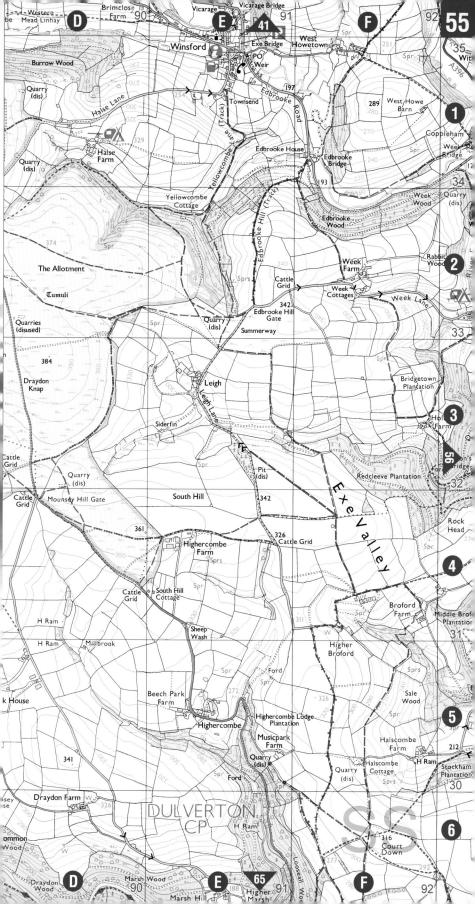

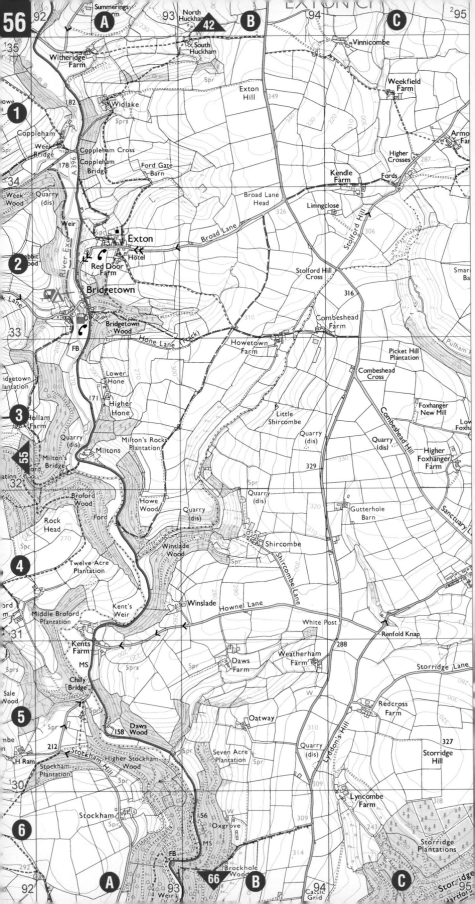

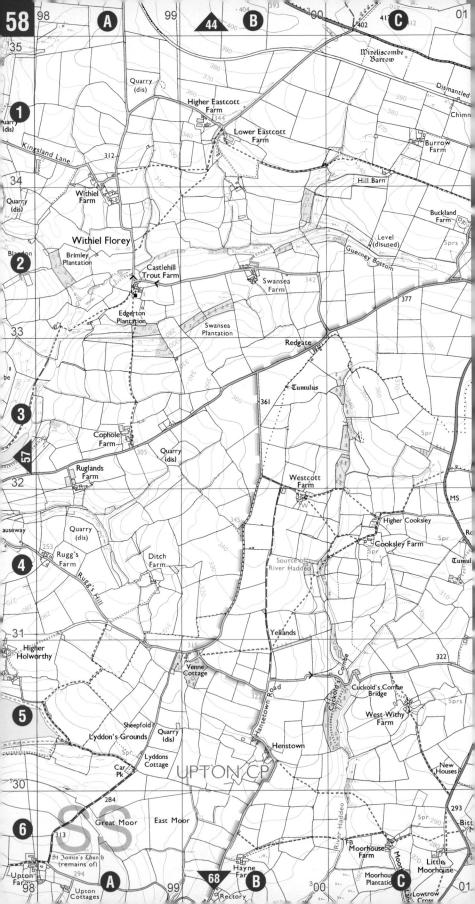

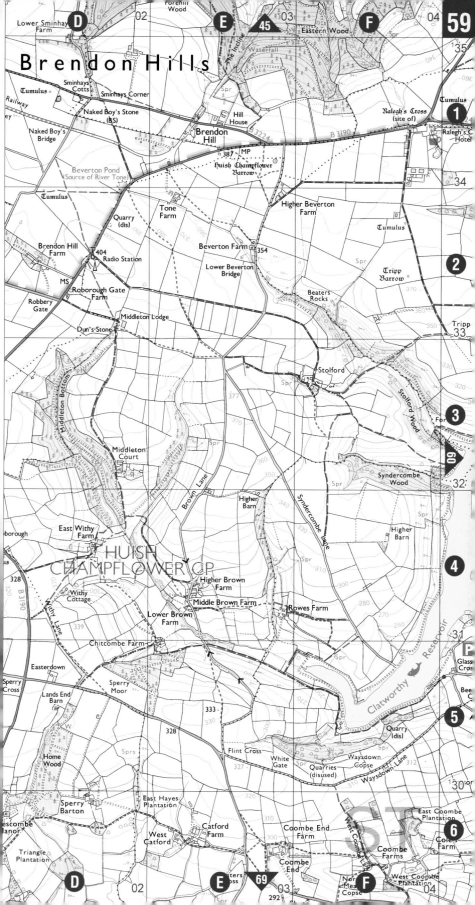

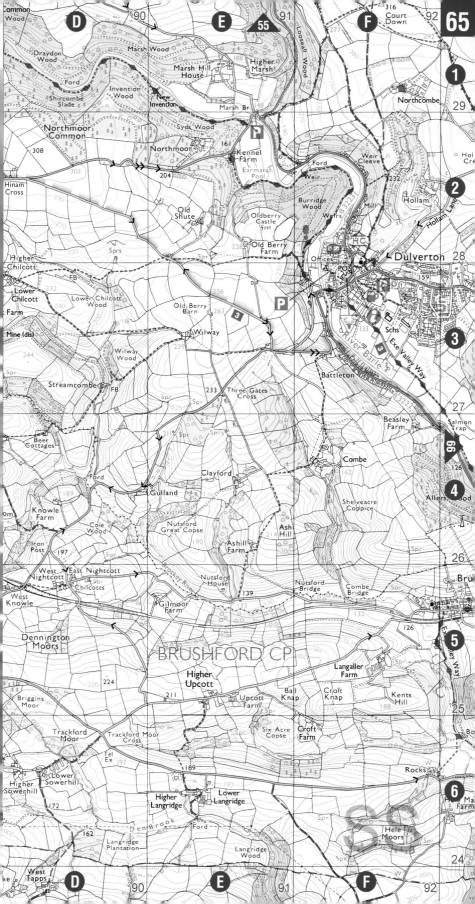

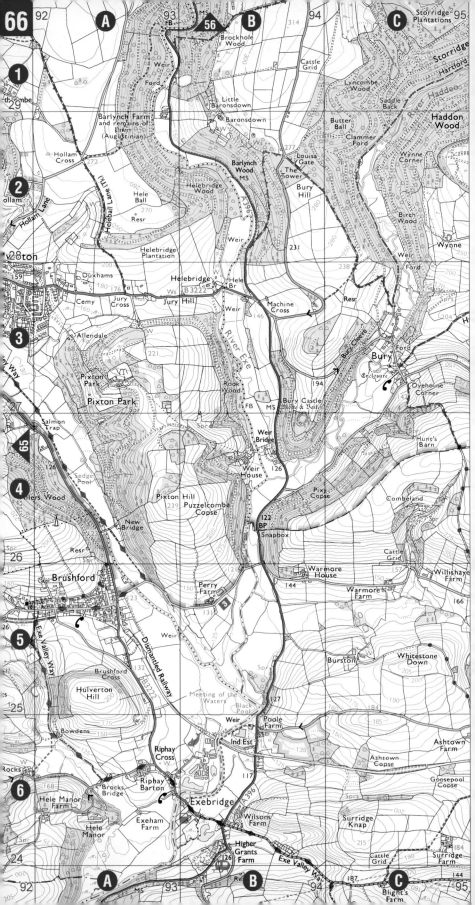

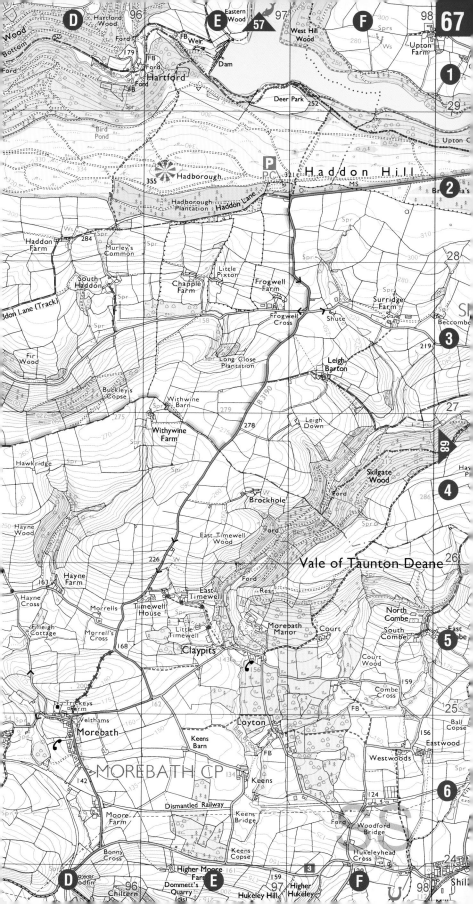